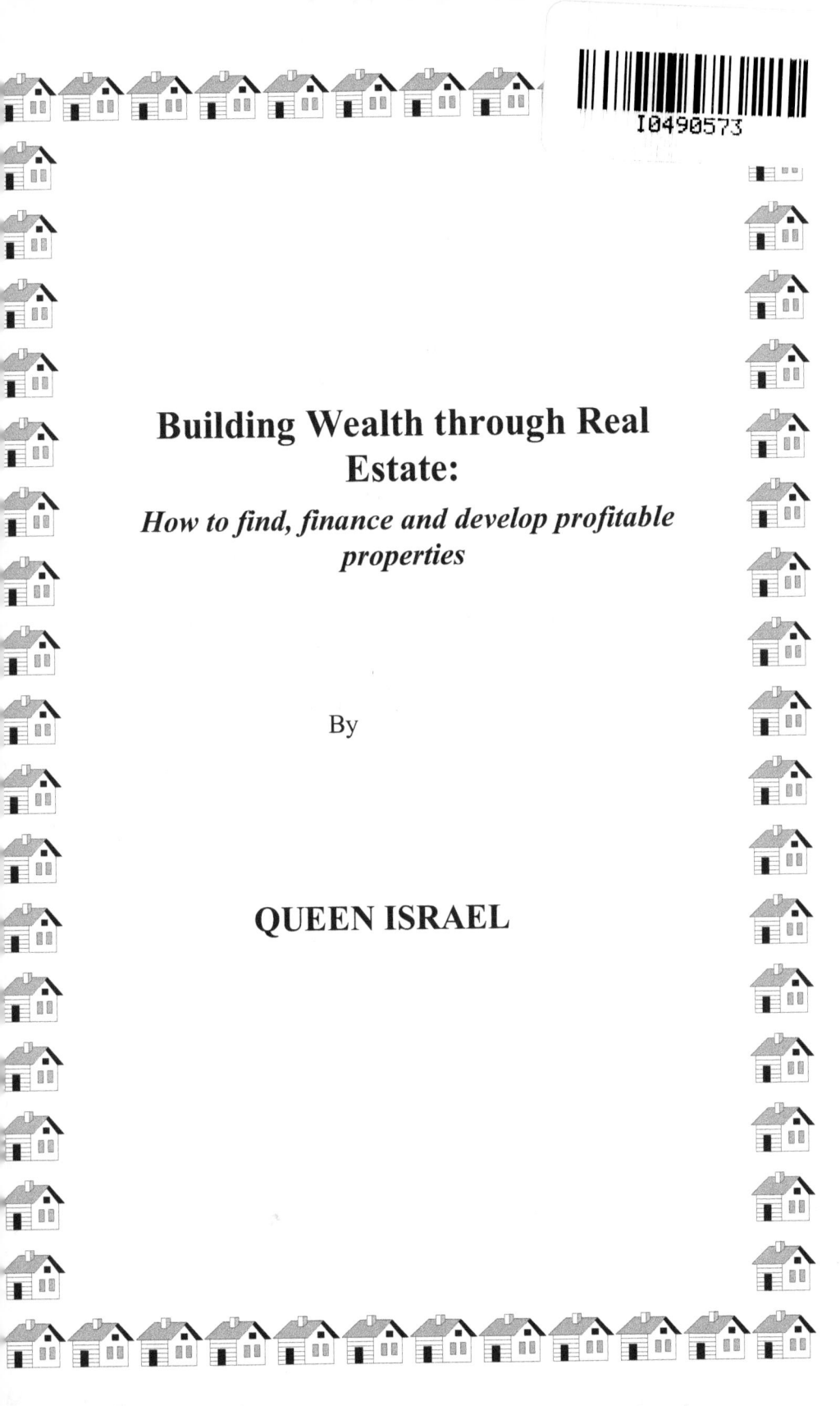

Building Wealth through Real Estate:

How to find, finance and develop profitable properties

By

QUEEN ISRAEL

Table of Contents

Chapter 1

Introduction to Real Estate Investing

Are you ready to take your finances to the next level? If so, you may want to consider real estate investing.

Real estate investing is a tried-and-true method for building wealth, and it can provide you with a steady stream of passive income for years to come.

But what exactly is real estate investing, and how does it work!

 In this chapter, you'll learn the basics of what real estate investing is and why it can be a great opportunity for building wealth.

Whether you're a seasoned investor or just starting out, this guide will provide you with a solid foundation for making informed decisions about your investments.

What is Real Estate Investing?

At its core, real estate investing is simply the act of buying, owning, managing, and selling real estate properties for profit. This can include a wide range of properties, from single-family homes to apartment buildings to commercial properties like office buildings or retail spaces.

The goal of real estate investing is to generate income from rent or other sources, as well as increase the value of the property over time.

For example, let's say you buy a single-family home for $200,000, and you rent it out for $1,500 a month. After paying your mortgage, taxes, and other expenses, you might be left with $500 in monthly profit. Over the course of a year, that's $6,000 in passive income! And if the value of the home increases over time, you'll see even more growth in your investment.

Why Invest in Real Estate?

There are many reasons why people choose to invest in real estate. Some of the most common benefits include:

- **Potential for passive income**: Renting out a property can provide a steady stream of income that can help supplement your regular earnings.
- **Appreciation**: Real estate values tend to rise over time, which can result in significant profits when you sell the property.
- **Tax benefits**: There are many tax benefits to owning real estate, including deductions for mortgage interest, property taxes, and depreciation.
- **Tangible asset**: Unlike stocks or bonds, real estate is a tangible asset that you can see, touch, and experience. This can make it a more stable investment option, especially in uncertain economic times.

The Real Estate Market

The real estate market can be influenced by a number of factors, including interest rates, economic growth, and supply and demand. When the economy is strong, demand for real estate tends to be high, which can drive up prices. Conversely, when the economy is weak, demand may drop, causing prices to fall.

However, despite fluctuations in the market, real estate has historically shown steady growth over time, making it a good investment option for the long term.

Real estate investing can be a great way to build wealth and secure your financial future.

Real Estate Investing in Action

Now that you have a basic understanding of what real estate investing is and why it can be a great opportunity, let's take a look at some real-life examples.

Meet Jane, a successful business owner who is looking for a way to invest her money and build wealth for the future. After doing her research, she decides to invest in a small apartment building. She buys the building for $1 million and rents out the units for a total of $10,000 a month. After paying her mortgage, taxes, and other expenses, Jane is left with $5,000 in monthly profit. That's an extra $60,000 a year in passive income! And over time, as the value of the building increases and her tenants renew their leases, Jane's wealth continues to grow.

Another Case study is Tom, a recent retiree who is looking for a way to generate income in retirement. He decides to invest in a few rental properties, starting with a single-family home in a growing neighborhood. He buys the home for $250,000 and rents it out for $1,800 a month. After paying his mortgage, taxes, and other expenses, Tom is left with $500 in monthly profit.

Different Types of Real Estate Investments

One of the great things about real estate investing is that there are many different ways to get involved. Here are a few of the most popular:

- **Residential Properties**: As we saw in our previous examples, residential properties include single-family homes, duplexes, triplexes, and small apartment buildings. These types of properties can provide a steady stream of passive income through rental payments.
- **Commercial Properties**: Commercial properties include office buildings, retail spaces, and other types of income-generating real estate. Investing in commercial properties can be more complex than investing in residential properties, but it can also be more lucrative. For example, let's say you invest in a commercial building that generates $100,000 a year in rent. After expenses, you're left with $50,000 in annual profit. That's a lot of passive income!
- **Real Estate Investment Trusts (REITs)**: REITs are companies that own and operate income-generating real estate. When you invest in a REIT, you're essentially buying a piece of the underlying real estate portfolio. REITs can be a great way to invest in real estate if you don't have the time or resources to manage your own properties.
- **Real Estate Crowdfunding:** Real estate crowdfunding is a newer form of real estate investing that allows you to invest in real estate properties alongside other investors. Let's say you want to invest in a new apartment building, but you don't have the money to buy it yourself. With real estate crowdfunding, you can invest as little as $100 and own a piece of the property alongside other investors.

The Importance of Location

One of the most important factors in real estate investing is location. The location of your property can have a big impact on its value, as well as its rental potential.

For example, let's say you have two rental properties: one in a great neighborhood with good schools and a low crime rate, and one in a high-crime area with struggling schools. Which one do you think will be more valuable and easier to rent out?

That's why it's important to do your research and choose your properties carefully. Look for properties in growing neighborhoods with good schools, low crime rates, and plenty of amenities.

You should also consider the local job market and the economy, as these can have a big impact on your rental potential.

The Importance of Property Management

Another important factor in real estate investing is property management. If you're going to be a successful real estate investor, you need to know how to manage your properties effectively. This includes finding and screening tenants, collecting rent, handling maintenance and repair issues, and more.

Let's say you buy a rental property and decide to manage it yourself. Everything is going well until one of your tenants moves out and you're left with a vacancy. If you don't know how to market your property, find a new tenant, and handle the move-in process, you could end up with a vacancy for several months. And that means you'll be losing out on rental income!

To avoid this, consider hiring a professional property management company.

A good property management company can handle all of the day-to-day tasks involved in managing your properties, freeing up your time to focus on growing your portfolio.

The Benefits of Real Estate Investing

Real estate investing has many benefits, including:

- **Appreciation**: Real estate can appreciate in value over time, providing you with a return on your investment. For example, if you buy a property for $200,000 and after 10 years it's worth $300,000. That's a 50% return on your investment!
- **Tax Benefits**: Real estate provides several tax benefits, including the ability to deduct mortgage interest, depreciation, and more. Let's say you have a rental property that generates $10,000 in rental income each year. After expenses, you have $5,000 in taxable income. If you have a tax bracket of 25%, you'll owe $1,250 in taxes. However, because of the tax benefits of real estate investing, you may be able to reduce your taxable income and pay less in taxes.
- **Passive Income**: Real estate can provide you with a steady stream of passive income through rental payments. For example, let's say you have a rental property that generates $1,000 in rent each month. That's $12,000 in passive income each year!
- **Diversification**: Real estate can help diversify your investment portfolio, reducing your overall risk. If you have a stock-heavy portfolio and the stock market crashes but if you have real estate investments, you may be able to weather the storm and protect your wealth.

The Risks of Real Estate Investing

Real estate investing also has its risks, including:

- **Market Fluctuations**: Real estate values can fluctuate based on a number of factors, including the local economy, interest rates, and more. For example, let's say you buy a property in a hot market and the market suddenly cools off. Your property value could decrease, leaving you with a loss.
- **Maintenance and Repair Costs**: Real estate requires regular maintenance and repair, which can be expensive. For example, let's say you have a rental property and one of your tenants reports a leaky roof. If you don't have the funds to repair the roof, you could be left with a vacancy and a loss of rental income.
- **Tenant Issues**: Dealing with tenants can be challenging, especially if you have a difficult tenant who doesn't pay rent or causes damage to the property. For example, let's say you have a tenant who stops paying rent and you have to go through the eviction process. This can be time-consuming and expensive.

Financing Your Real Estate Investments

There are many different types of real estate investments and financing options available. It's important to consider your personal financial situation and goals when choosing which type of investment and financing option is right for you. With the right approach, real estate investing can be a great way to build wealth and achieve your financial goals.

The several ways to finance your real estate investments include:

- **Cash**: If you have cash available, you can buy a property outright. For example, let's say you have $200,000 in cash and you want to buy a rental property. You can use your cash to purchase the property and start earning rental income right away.

- **Mortgages**: If you don't have cash available, you can use a mortgage to finance your real estate investment. For example, let's say you want to buy a rental property for $200,000 and you have a down payment of $40,000. You can get a mortgage for the remaining $160,000 and start earning rental income right away.
- **Partnerships**: If you don't have enough cash or can't qualify for a mortgage, you can partner with another investor. For example, let's say you have $40,000 and you want to buy a rental property for $200,000. You can partner with another investor who has $160,000 and together you can purchase the property.

Chapter 2
Understanding the Real Estate Market

Real estate markets are constantly changing, and it's important to have a good understanding of the market in order to make informed investment decisions.

Real estate is one of the largest and most dynamic markets in the world, and understanding how it works is crucial for anyone looking to invest in property.

The Real Estate Market:

The real estate market is essentially the buying and selling of properties, such as homes, apartments, commercial buildings, and land. The market is driven by supply and demand, just like any other market. When demand for properties is high, prices go up. When demand is low, prices go down.

The supply of properties is determined by the number of properties available for sale, as well as the rate of new construction. On the other hand, demand is influenced by a variety of factors, including interest rates, the economy, and population growth.

How it Works:

The real estate market operates through a network of agents, brokers, and developers, who buy, sell, and develop properties. When a property owner wants to sell their property, they usually hire a real estate agent to list the property for sale. The agent markets the property to potential buyers, holds open houses, and negotiates offers.

Once a buyer and seller agree on a price, the transaction is finalized through a contract, and the buyer takes ownership of the property. The buyer typically pays a down payment, and then makes monthly mortgage payments to repay the loan used to purchase the property.

Practical Examples:

1. Consider the case of a young couple, John and Sarah, who are looking to buy their first home. They work with a real estate agent to find a suitable property, and after several months of searching, they find a three-bedroom home in a nice neighborhood that meets their needs and budget. They negotiate the price with the seller, and after several weeks, they sign the contract and take ownership of the home.
2. Another example is the case of a successful business owner, Bob, who is looking to invest in commercial real estate. He works with a real estate broker to find a suitable property, such as an office building or shopping center. After evaluating several properties, Bob decides to purchase a large office building in a high-traffic area. He secures financing, and after several months, he takes ownership of the property and begins to lease out the office spaces to tenants.
3. Meet Tom, a recent college graduate who's eager to start investing in real estate. He begins by researching the market and talking to experienced real estate investors. Tom learns about the importance of location and decides to focus on finding properties in up-and-coming neighborhoods. After several months of

searching, he finds a small apartment building in a neighborhood that's undergoing gentrification. He negotiates a good price for the building and secures financing. Tom becomes a landlord and starts earning passive income from rent. Over time, as the neighborhood continues to improve, the value of the property increases, and Tom's investment grows.

4. Consider the story of Jane, a single mother who wants to invest in real estate to secure her financial future. She starts by learning as much as she can about the market and talking to real estate professionals. Jane decides to focus on finding properties in need of renovation, which she can buy, fix up, and sell for a profit. After several months of searching, she finds a run-down house in a desirable neighborhood. She buys the house, does some renovations, and puts it back on the market. The house sells quickly for a substantial profit, and Jane uses the money to purchase another property to renovate and sell. This becomes her business model, and she becomes a successful real estate investor.

5. Meet Alex and his friend Ben, who are looking to invest in real estate together. They start by researching the market and talking to real estate professionals. They decide to focus on finding properties to rent out and generate passive income. After several months of searching, they find a four-unit apartment building in a good location. They negotiate a good price for the building, secure financing, and become landlords. Over time, as the value of the property increases, so do their passive income and their investment grow?

These examples illustrate how the real estate market operates and how people can participate in the market as buyers, sellers, or investors.

Key elements of a real estate market include.

1. *Supply and Demand*

The law of supply and demand is a fundamental principle that drives the real estate market. When the demand for real estate is high, prices typically rise. Conversely, when demand is low, prices typically fall.

For example, let's say you live in a city with a strong economy and job market. As more people move to the city, demand for housing increases. As demand increases, so do home prices.

On the other hand, if the city's economy slows down and people start moving out, demand for housing decreases and home prices fall.

Economic Indicators

Economic indicators can have a significant impact on the real estate market. When interest rates are low, it's typically easier for people to obtain mortgages, which can increase demand for housing and drive up home prices.

Conversely, when interest rates are high, it can be more difficult for people to obtain mortgages, which can decrease demand for housing and drive down home prices.

Another important economic indicator is the job market. When the job market is strong, people are more likely to have stable income and the ability to afford housing, which can increase demand for housing and drive up home prices. However, when the job market is weak, people are less likely to have stable income and the ability to afford housing, which can decrease demand for housing and drive down home prices.

Local Market Conditions

Local market conditions, such as the availability of housing, local zoning regulations, and the condition of local infrastructure, can also impact the real estate market.

For example, if there's a shortage of housing in a city, demand for housing will likely be high, which can drive up home prices. On the other hand, if there's an oversupply of housing, demand will likely be low, which can drive down home prices.

Similarly, local zoning regulations can impact the real estate market by affecting the supply of housing. For Instance, if a city implements strict zoning regulations that limit the development of new housing, it can limit the supply of housing and drive up home prices.

More so, the condition of local infrastructure, such as roads, schools, and public transportation, can also impact the real estate market. If a city invests in improving its infrastructure, it can make the city more attractive to potential homebuyers, which can increase demand for housing and drive up home prices.

Understanding the real estate market is crucial for making informed investment decisions. By paying attention to supply and demand, economic indicators, and local market conditions, you can make better investment decisions and increase your chances of success in real estate investing.

Practical examples to help illustrate the concepts of supply and demand, economic indicators, and local market conditions in the real estate market.

Supply and Demand:

1. A classic example of the impact of supply and demand on the real estate market is the housing market in San Francisco. As the tech industry boomed in the city, demand for housing increased, driving up home prices. However, with strict zoning regulations and limited land available for new housing development, the supply of housing was unable to keep up with demand, causing home prices to soar.
2. Another example is a small town that was once a popular tourist destination. As more and more tourists flocked to the town, demand for vacation rentals increased, driving up prices. However, as the town's popularity waned and tourists stopped coming, demand for vacation rentals decreased, causing prices to fall.

Economic Indicators:

1. In 2008, the Great Recession hit and many people lost their jobs, causing a decrease in demand for housing and driving down home prices. In addition, the Federal Reserve raised interest rates, making it more difficult for people to obtain mortgages, further exacerbating the decrease in demand for housing.
2. On the other hand, in the mid-2010s, the economy began to recover and job growth picked up, causing an increase in demand for housing and driving up home prices. Additionally, the Federal Reserve lowered interest rates, making it easier for people to obtain mortgages, further fueling the increase in demand for housing.

Local Market Conditions:

1. A prime example of the impact of local market conditions on the real estate market is the housing market in New

York City. The city has strict zoning regulations that limit the development of new housing, causing a shortage of housing and driving up home prices.

2. In another example, a small town in the Midwest invested in improving its infrastructure, such as roads and public transportation, making the town more attractive to potential homebuyers. This increased demand for housing and drove up home prices.

The Different Types of Real Estate Properties:

1. **Residential Properties**: Meet Sarah, a young professional who's looking to invest in real estate. After researching the market and talking to real estate professionals, Sarah decides to focus on residential properties. She starts by looking for single-family homes in desirable neighborhoods. After several months of searching, she finds a charming three-bedroom house in a good location. She negotiates a good price for the house, secures financing, and becomes a homeowner. Over time, as the value of the property increases, Sarah's investment grows, and she has the option to rent out the house to generate passive income.

2. **Commercial Properties:** John, a successful business owner who wants to diversify his investments. After researching the market and talking to real estate professionals, John decides to focus on commercial properties. He starts by looking for retail spaces in busy shopping centers. After several months of searching, he finds a well-located retail space that he can lease to a successful business. Over time, as the value of the property increases, so does John's passive income, and his investment grows.

3. **Industrial Properties:** Meet Jake, an engineer who's looking to invest in real estate. After researching the market

and talking to real estate professionals, Jake decides to focus on industrial properties. He starts by looking for warehouse spaces in growing industrial areas. After several months of searching, he finds a large warehouse space that he can lease to a successful company. Over time, as the value of the property increases, so does Jake's passive income, and his investment grows.

4. **Mixed-Use Properties**: Consider the story of Lauren, a young entrepreneur who wants to invest in real estate. After researching the market and talking to real estate professionals, Lauren decides to focus on mixed-use properties. She starts by looking for properties that include residential, commercial, and industrial spaces. After several months of searching, she finds a large building that includes retail spaces, office spaces, and warehouse spaces. She negotiates a good price for the building, secures financing, and becomes a landlord. Over time, as the value of the property increases, so does Lauren's passive income, and her investment grows.

These examples demonstrate the different types of real estate properties that you can invest in, each with its own unique benefits and risks. Whether you're a young professional, a successful business owner, an engineer, or an entrepreneur, there's a real estate property that's right for you.

5. **Vacation Properties**: Meet Tom and Jane, a young couple who want to invest in real estate. After researching the market and talking to real estate professionals, they decide to focus on vacation properties. They start by looking for properties in popular tourist destinations. After several months of searching, they find a charming beachfront condo in a good location. They negotiate a good price for the condo, secure financing, and become part-time homeowners. Over time, as the value of the property

increases, Tom and Jane's investment grows, and they have the option to rent out the condo to generate passive income.

This example demonstrates the benefits of investing in vacation properties, which can offer a combination of personal use and rental income. Whether you're a young couple, a family, or a retiree, there's a vacation property that's right for you. Just like with any other type of real estate investment, it's important to do your research, work with a professional, and carefully consider the potential

benefits and risks before making a decision.

6. **Multi-Family Properties**: Meet Mike, a young investor who wants to invest in real estate. After researching the market and talking to real estate professionals, he decides to focus on multi-family properties. He starts by looking for properties with multiple units, such as apartments or townhouses. After several months of searching, he finds a well-located apartment building with several units. He negotiates a good price for the building, secures financing, and becomes a landlord. Over time, as the value of the property increases, so does Mike's passive income, and his investment grows.

This example demonstrates the benefits of investing in multi-family properties, which can provide a large scale rental income. Just like with any other type of real estate investment, it's important to do your research, work with a professional, and carefully consider the potential benefits and risks before making a decision.

Chapter 3
Analyzing Real Estate Market Trends

Understanding the real estate market trends is crucial for making informed investment decisions. Real estate market trends can be analyzed at the local, national, and global level, and each level offers different insights and opportunities. In this chapter, we'll explore the different ways to analyze real estate market trends and how you can use this information to your advantage.

1. **Local Market Trends**: Understanding the local real estate market is essential for making informed investment decisions. To analyze the local real estate market, you should consider factors such as population growth, job growth, and the local economy. For example, if you are investing in a market with a growing population and a strong economy, you can expect property values to increase and rental demand to be high. On the other hand, if the local economy is weak and the population is declining, you may face challenges in finding renters and may experience lower property values. Additionally, you should also be aware of local zoning laws and regulations, which can affect the development of new properties and property values.

    Meet Susan, a real estate agent who specializes in the local market. Susan has a deep understanding of the local real estate market and knows what's happening in her area. For example, she knows that the demand for single-family homes is high, and that prices have been steadily increasing over the past few years. She also knows that new developments are planned for the area, which will likely drive up property values even further. By staying informed about local real estate trends, Susan is better able to serve her clients and make informed investment decisions.

2. **National Market Trends:** Understanding national real estate market trends can give you a broad view of the real estate market as a whole and help you make informed investment decisions. Some of the key indicators to look at when analyzing national market trends include interest rates, housing starts, and home sales data. For example, if interest rates are low and housing starts are increasing, it may indicate a strong real estate market, which can be a good opportunity for investment. On the other hand, if interest rates are high and housing starts are declining, it may indicate a weak real estate market and may not be a good time to invest.

   Meet Bob, a real estate investor who is interested in national market trends. Bob knows that the real estate market is a cycle and that it's important to understand where the market is in the cycle in order to make informed investment decisions. For example, Bob knows that the national real estate market is currently in an upswing, which means that property values are increasing, and that it's a good time to invest. By staying informed about national real estate trends, Bob is able to make informed investment decisions and maximize his returns.

3. **Global Market Trends**: The global real estate market is interconnected, and it's important to understand global trends to make informed investment decisions. Some of the factors to consider when analyzing global real estate trends include economic growth, political stability, and cultural differences. For example, if the economy is growing in a particular country, it may be a good opportunity for investment, as this may lead to an increase in property values and rental demand. On the other hand, if a country is facing political instability or cultural differences, it may not

be a good time to invest, as these factors can affect the real estate market negatively.

Meet Sarah, a real estate investor who is interested in global market trends. Sarah knows that the global real estate market is interconnected, and that it's important to understand what's happening in other parts of the world in order to make informed investment decisions. For example, Sarah knows that the real estate market in Asia is currently growing, and that there are many opportunities for investment. By staying informed about global real estate trends, Sarah is able to make informed investment decisions and capitalize on the best opportunities.

Analyzing real estate market trends at the local, national, and global level is crucial for making informed investment decisions. . By staying informed and considering factors such as population growth, job growth, local economy, interest rates, housing starts, home sales data, economic growth, political stability, and cultural differences, you can make better investment decisions and build wealth through real estate.

Chapter 4
Finding the Right Properties

As a real estate investor, finding the right properties to invest in is one of the most important aspects of building wealth through real estate. To find the right properties, you need to consider your investment goals, risk tolerance, and the real estate market trends.

1. **Identify Your Investment Goals**: The first step in finding the right properties is to identify your investment goals. Are you looking for long-term wealth building, steady passive income, or quick profits? Knowing your investment goals will help you narrow down your search and focus on properties that align with your goals.

2. **Consider Your Risk Tolerance**: Real estate investing involves some level of risk, and it's important to consider your risk tolerance before making an investment. For example, if you have a low risk tolerance, you may want to consider investing in established properties with a proven track record of generating steady income. On the other hand, if you have a high risk tolerance, you may want to consider investing in properties that have the potential for high returns but also come with a higher level of risk.

3. **Analyze Market Trends**: Before making an investment, it's important to understand the real estate market trends in the area where you are considering investing. For example, if the market is experiencing growth and there is a high demand for rental properties, it may be a good time to invest. On the other hand, if the market is slowing down and there is a low demand

for rental properties, it may not be the best time to invest.

4. **Network with Real Estate Professionals**: Networking with real estate professionals such as agents, brokers, and contractors can be a valuable resource when searching for properties. These professionals can provide you with information on available properties, market trends, and other important details that can help you make informed **investment decisions.**

5. **Use Real Estate Technology**: Technology has revolutionized the real estate industry and has made it easier to find properties. There are many online tools and platforms available that can help you search for properties, analyze market trends, and compare properties to find the best investment opportunities.

6. **Drive By and Do Your Own Research**: Once you have identified potential properties, it's a good idea to drive by the area and get a feel for the neighborhood. This can help you determine if the location is a good fit for your investment goals. You can also research crime rates, local schools, and other important factors that can affect the value of the property and the demand for rental properties in the area.

7. **Utilize Online Real Estate Listings**: Online real estate listings, such as Zillow, Redfin, and Realtor.com, can be a great resource for finding properties for investment. These websites allow you to search for properties by location, price range, and other criteria, making it easier to find properties that meet your investment goals. You can also research property values, rental rates, and the demand for rental properties in your desired location using these websites.

8. **Attend Real Estate Investment Meetings**: Attending real estate investment meetings, such as local real estate investor associations (REIA), can be a great way to meet other real estate investors and learn about

investment opportunities. These meetings provide a platform for real estate investors to network, share information, and find properties for investment. You can also attend real estate investment seminars and workshops to learn about the latest market trends and investment strategies.

9. **Utilize Real Estate Auctions**: Real estate auctions can be a great way to find investment properties. Auctions provide an opportunity to purchase properties at a discounted price and often have a large selection of properties available for sale. Before attending an auction, it's important to research the properties that will be up for sale, as well as the terms and conditions of the auction.

10. **Connect with Distressed Property Owners**: Connecting with distressed property owners, such as those facing foreclosure, can be a great way to find investment properties. These property owners are often motivated to sell their properties quickly, and they may be willing to sell the properties at a discounted price. You can find distressed property owners by searching online, contacting local real estate agents, or attending real estate investment meetings.

11. **Utilize Property Management Companies**: Property management companies can be a great resource for finding investment properties. They often have a large portfolio of properties available for rent, and they can help you identify properties that meet your investment goals. Property management companies can also provide you with valuable information about rental rates, property values, and the demand for rental properties in the area.

12. **Work with a Real Estate Agent**: Working with a real estate agent can be a great way to find investment properties. Real estate agents have a wealth of knowledge about the local market and can help you

identify properties that meet your investment goals. They can also provide you with valuable information about property values, rental rates, and the demand for rental properties in the area. By working with a real estate agent, you can have access to properties that may not be publicly listed, increasing your chances of finding the right properties for investment.

13. **Foreclosures:** Foreclosures can be a great source of investment properties, but it's important to understand the process and the risks involved. You can attend local foreclosure auctions, search for properties listed for sale through the government, or work with a real estate agent who specializes in foreclosures.

14. **Real Estate Investment Trusts (REITs):** If you're not interested in owning physical real estate, you can still invest in real estate through REITs. REITs are publicly traded companies that own, manage, and often finance income-producing real estate properties. You can purchase shares of REITs through a brokerage account, just like you would with stocks or bonds.

15. **Look for Properties with Potential for Added Value**: Properties that have the potential for added value, such as properties that need renovations or properties in up-and-coming neighborhoods, can be a good investment opportunity. By adding value to a property, you can increase its rental income and resale value, and potentially earn higher returns on your investment.

16. **Check the Property's Condition**: Before making an investment, it's important to inspect the property and check its condition. This can help you identify any potential problems or issues that may need to be addressed and determine the cost of repairs and renovations. You can also consider hiring a professional home inspector to thoroughly inspect the property and provide you with a detailed report.

17. **Consider the Potential Rent**: When evaluating a potential property, it's important to consider the potential rent. Research the rental rates for similar properties in the area to determine if the property will generate enough income to cover your expenses and provide you with a positive cash flow.
18. **Negotiate the Purchase Price**: Once you have found a property that meets your investment goals and criteria, it's important to negotiate the purchase price. You can work with a real estate agent or broker to negotiate the purchase price and terms, and ensure that you are getting the best deal possible.

Identifying profitable properties can be a challenging task, but with the right tools and techniques, it can be done with ease.

Here are some tips for identifying profitable properties:

1. **Location, location, location:** The old adage holds true, the location of a property is crucial to its profitability. Look for properties in up-and-coming areas with a strong rental demand, near transportation hubs, and good schools.
2. **Conduct a thorough property inspection**: Before making an offer on a property, it's important to conduct a thorough inspection. This will give you a good idea of any necessary repairs or renovations and will help you determine the true value of the property.
3. **Do your research on property values**: Research recent sales in the area to get a sense of the market value of properties in the area. You can use online real estate websites, talk to local real estate agents, or consult with a professional appraiser.
4. **Consider the property's cash flow**: Cash flow is the amount of money you have left over each month after all

expenses have been paid. The more positive the cash flow, the more profitable the property will be.

5. **Know your numbers**: It's important to have a good understanding of your expenses, including property taxes, insurance, maintenance costs, and mortgage payments. You can use an online property analysis tool or consult with a real estate professional to help you with this.

6. **Consider your goals and timeline**: Your investment goals and timeline will play a big role in determining whether a property is a good investment. If your goal is long-term wealth creation, you may be willing to hold onto a property for a longer period of time, even if it doesn't generate much income in the short-term. If you're looking to generate quick cash, you may want to focus on properties with high rental demand.

Here's a practical example:

Let's say you come across a property in a desirable neighborhood with a price tag of $200,000. After conducting a thorough inspection, you determine that you need to spend $30,000 on renovations to bring the property up to market standards. You research recent sales in the area and find that similar properties are renting for $1,500 per month. With your monthly expenses estimated at $1,000, you calculate that the property will generate $500 in positive cash flow each month. Based on these numbers, you determine that this property is a good investment and move forward with the purchase.

Practical Examples to highlight the different methods that real estate investors can use to identify profitable properties

1. Sarah, a real estate investor, was always fascinated by the potential for high returns in real estate. One day, she stumbled upon a run-down, multi-unit building in a

low-income neighborhood. Despite its appearance, Sarah saw the potential for profitability. She conducted market research and found that the area was undergoing gentrification, and the prices of similar properties in the area were rapidly increasing. Sarah purchased the building, renovated it, and successfully raised the rent prices, turning it into a profitable investment.

2. Jake, another real estate investor, was always on the lookout for undervalued properties. He would spend hours analyzing market data and looking at property records to identify properties that were selling below their market value. One day, he came across a property that had been on the market for months and was selling at a price that was well below its market value. Jake quickly made an offer and purchased the property, which he then flipped for a profit after making some cosmetic renovations.

3. Maria, a new real estate investor, was seeking her first investment property. She was recommended by a friend to attend local real estate events and network with other investors. At one such event, she met an experienced investor who shared his insights on the local market and helped her identify a potential opportunity. Maria ended up purchasing a multi-unit property that was in need of some repairs, but had a lot of potential for growth in rent prices. She made the necessary renovations, and within a few months, was able to lease all units at higher prices, making a significant profit on her investment.

4. Mark, a real estate investor, was always looking for the next hot real estate market. He heard that a new shopping mall was being built in a previously underdeveloped area and decided to invest in a rental property there. However, he failed to conduct proper market research and missed important details about the area, such as high crime rates and limited job

opportunities. As a result, Mark had difficulty finding tenants for his property, and the rent prices were lower than he had anticipated. He eventually had to sell the property at a loss.

5. Karen, a seasoned real estate investor, learned from her previous mistakes and placed a strong emphasis on location and market research. She researched different neighborhoods and found one that was undergoing revitalization, with new businesses and job opportunities popping up. She also made sure to check the local crime rates and transportation options before making her investment. Karen's due diligence paid off as her rental property was in high demand, and she was able to charge premium rent prices.

6. Jack, another real estate investor, was looking to invest in a vacation rental property. He had a specific location in mind, but before making his investment, he conducted thorough market research. He looked at tourist patterns, seasonal fluctuations in rental demand, and the competition in the area. Based on his research, Jack was able to identify the best time to purchase the property and set competitive rental prices, resulting in a profitable investment.

Chapter 4
Financing Your Investments

When it comes to real estate investing, having the right financing can make all the difference. Investing in real estate is a capital-intensive venture and securing financing is one of the most crucial aspects of the process. In this chapter, we'll explore the various options for financing your real estate investments and how to make the best choice for your financial goals and circumstances.

1. Traditional Bank Loans / Conventional Mortgages

The most straightforward way to finance a real estate investment is through a traditional bank loan. You can obtain a mortgage for a primary residence, vacation home or investment property. The requirements and terms of these loans can vary depending on the type of property and your credit history, but they typically require a substantial down payment and a good credit score.

Example 1: Sarah is a first-time real estate investor looking to purchase a rental property. She has saved up a substantial down payment and has a good credit score, so she decides to finance the purchase through a traditional bank loan. She works with a lender to find a loan with a competitive interest rate and flexible repayment terms that meet her needs.

2. Hard Money Loans

If you're looking for a faster and more flexible way to finance your real estate investments, you might consider a hard money loan. These loans are provided by private investors or firms, and they're often used by real estate investors for short-term financing for fix-and-flip projects. The requirements for hard money loans are typically less stringent than for traditional bank loans, but the interest rates can be higher and the repayment terms shorter.

Example 2: Joe is an experienced real estate investor who specializes in flipping properties. He's found a great opportunity to purchase a fixer-upper and needs financing quickly. He decides to go with a hard money loan, which allows him to close on the property quickly and get started on renovations. The high interest rate on the loan is offset by the profits he expects to make on the sale of the property.

3. Home Equity Loans

If you already own a home, you can use the equity in that property to finance your real estate investments. Home equity loans allow you to borrow against the value of your home, using it as collateral. Home equity loans typically have lower interest rates than other types of loans and can be a good choice if you have a lot of equity in your home and a good credit score.

Example 3: Susan has been a homeowner for many years and has built up a significant amount of equity in her home. She's interested in investing in real estate, but doesn't have the cash on hand to make a down payment on a rental property. She decides to take out a home equity loan, using the equity in her home as collateral. This allows her to finance the purchase of a rental property without dipping into her savings.

4. Partnering with Other Investors

Another option for financing your real estate investments is to partner with other investors. This can be a great way to pool resources and share the risk, but it also requires careful consideration of the terms of the partnership and the strengths and weaknesses of your partners.

Example 4: Tom and David are both real estate investors, but they have different areas of expertise. Tom is an expert in finding great properties, while David has experience in property management and financing. They decide to partner on a real estate investment, with Tom finding the property and David financing the purchase and managing the property. This partnership allows them to combine their strengths and make a more profitable investment than they could on their own.

5. Lines of Credit

Lines of credit are a type of financing that allows you to draw funds as needed, up to a specified limit. These loans are often used by real estate investors to cover short-term costs, such as down payments or closing costs. Lines of credit typically have lower interest rates compared to other financing options, but they also come with stricter underwriting criteria.

Example 5:

John, a real estate investor, had been searching for his next investment property for months. He finally found a promising rental property in a rapidly growing neighborhood and was ready to make an offer. However, he realized that he didn't have enough cash on hand to cover the down payment and closing costs. John decided to *apply for a line of credit from his bank. He was approved for a $50,000 line of credit, which he used to cover the costs associated with the purchase of the property. With the help of the line of credit, John was able to secure his next investment property and start building wealth through real estate.*

6. **Real Estate Investment Trusts (REITs)** - REITs are investment vehicles that allow individuals to invest in real estate without having to buy a property themselves. Instead, they purchase shares in the trust, which in turn invests in a portfolio of real estate assets.

7. **Crowdfunding** - Crowdfunding is a newer form of financing that involves pooling small investments from a large number of people to fund a single project or investment. Crowdfunding platforms, such as Fundrise and RealtyMogul, allow investors to get involved in real estate investing with as little as $500.

Chapter 5
How to Get a Mortgage Loan

Mortgage loans are a popular way to finance real estate investments. In this chapter, we'll explore the process of getting a mortgage loan and what you need to know before applying.

First thing first, let's define what a mortgage loan is. A mortgage loan is a loan used to purchase a property. The property is used as collateral for the loan, and the lender holds a lien on the property until the loan is repaid.

Now, let's say you've found the perfect investment property, and you're ready to apply for a mortgage loan.

Here's what you need to know:

1. Determine How Much You Can Afford Before you start looking for a mortgage loan, it's important to determine how much you can afford to borrow. You can use online mortgage calculators to get an idea of your monthly payment and how much you can afford to borrow. Keep in mind that you'll also need to factor in property taxes, insurance, and any other expenses related to owning the property.
2. Choose the Right LenderL: There are many lenders to choose from when it comes to mortgage loans. Some of the most common include banks, credit unions, and online lenders. Do your research to find a lender that offers the best terms and interest rates for your needs.

3. Pre-Approval Getting pre-approved for a mortgage loan is a crucial step in the process. A pre-approval is a preliminary assessment of your creditworthiness and shows that you are a serious buyer. It also gives you a clear understanding of how much you can borrow and helps you to avoid overspending.
4. Gathering Documentation: To apply for a mortgage loan, you'll need to provide the lender with a variety of documentation. This may include your credit report, proof of income, and proof of assets. Be prepared to provide all of the required documentation to make the process as smooth as possible.
5. Closing the Deal Once your loan is approved, you'll need to sign a mortgage agreement and close the deal. The closing process involves the transfer of ownership of the property, the payment of any closing costs, and the disbursement of funds to the seller.

Let's take a look at a practical example of how to get a mortgage loan:

Tom and Sarah are looking to invest in a rental property. They have been saving up for years and have a solid credit history. They have done their research and have found a lender that offers competitive interest rates and flexible repayment terms.

They start the pre-approval process and provide the lender with all of the required documentation. The lender assesses their creditworthiness and determines that they are a good fit for a mortgage loan.

Tom and Sarah are approved for a mortgage loan and they close the deal on the property. They make a down payment, and their monthly mortgage payments are automatically deducted from their bank account. They are now proud owners of a rental property that will generate income for years to come.

Here are some more practical examples of getting a mortgage loan:

Example 1: Maria is a first-time homebuyer who has saved up for a down payment but doesn't have much credit history. She finds a mortgage broker who specializes in working with first-time homebuyers and has a strong reputation. The broker helps Maria understand the different types of mortgage loans available and guides her through the application process. After reviewing her finances, the broker is able to secure a loan with a good interest rate for Maria, who is now able to purchase her dream home.

Example 2: John and Sarah are a young couple looking to buy their first home. They've done their research and found a neighborhood that's up-and-coming and close to their work. However, they are self-employed and don't have traditional W-2 forms to show their income. They find a lender who specializes in working with self-employed borrowers and are able to secure a loan using their tax returns, bank statements, and other financial documents. The lender takes into account the stability and growth of their business and approves them for a loan, which allows John and Sarah to purchase their first home.

Example 3: David is a seasoned real estate investor who is looking to finance a rental property. He has a good credit score and a solid portfolio of rental properties, but he doesn't have the cash to make a down payment on a new property. He finds a lender who offers a no-money-down loan, which allows him to finance the property and get a return on investment right away. David is now able to grow his rental property portfolio and build his wealth through real estate.

These are just a few examples of how individuals have used different financing options to pursue their real estate investment goals. By working with experienced professionals and understanding the various financing options available, you too can make your real estate investment dreams a reality.

Chapter 5
Developing Your Properties

Developing real estate properties is a great way to increase the value of your investment and generate long-term wealth. However, it's important to understand that this process can be complex, time-consuming and requires significant capital. In this chapter, we'll explore the steps involved in developing properties and the key considerations to keep in mind as you move forward.

Step 1: Identifying Your Investment Strategy

Before you begin developing a property, you need to have a clear investment strategy in place. This will help you to identify the type of property you're looking for and the target market you're trying to reach. For example, you might decide to focus on multi-family properties in a growing city that's attracting young professionals.

Step 2: Conducting Market Research

Once you've identified your investment strategy, it's important to conduct thorough market research. This will give you a better understanding of the local real estate market and help you to identify potential development opportunities. You should consider factors such as the local economy, population trends, and the demand for rental properties in the area.

Step 3: Securing Funding

Developing properties requires significant capital, so you'll need to secure funding for your project. This may include a combination of your own savings, a mortgage loan, and investment from partners or investors. Make sure you have a solid financial plan in place before you start the development process.

Step 4: Hiring a Team of Professionals

Developing properties requires the expertise of a wide range of professionals, including architects, contractors, and real estate agents. You'll need to work with these professionals to ensure that your project runs smoothly and that you're able to achieve your desired outcomes. It's important to hire the right team, so be sure to take the time to research and interview potential candidates.

Step 5: Developing Your Properties

The actual process of developing properties can be complex, so it's important to have a clear plan in place. You'll need to manage construction, marketing, and leasing, and be prepared to handle any unexpected challenges that may arise. With the right team in place, however, developing properties can be a rewarding experience that generates significant returns over the long-term.

Practical Examples:

1. *Sarah is a real estate investor who has decided to focus on developing multi-family properties in a growing city. She starts by conducting thorough market research to understand the local economy and the demand for rental properties. With her investment strategy in place, she secures funding from a combination of her own savings and*

a mortgage loan. She hires a team of professionals, including architects, contractors, and real estate agents, to help her with the development process. After several months of hard work, Sarah's properties are completed and she's able to start generating rental income.

2. *John is a seasoned real estate investor who has decided to develop a high-end condominium complex in a popular tourist destination. He starts by conducting market research to understand the local real estate market and the demand for luxury properties. With his investment strategy in place, he secures funding from a group of investors. He hires a team of professionals, including architects, contractors, and real estate agents, to help him with the development process. After several years of hard work, John's condominium complex is completed and he's able to start generating significant returns from the sale of the units.*

How to develop and renovate properties:

Developing and renovating properties can be a lucrative venture, but it also requires a great deal of time, effort, and capital. In order to succeed, it's important to have a clear plan in place from the outset. Here are a few practical examples of how to develop and renovate properties:

1. **Start with a plan**: Before you even begin to look for properties, it's important to have a clear plan in place. This should include a budget, a timeline, and a list of the specific improvements you want to make. You should also have a good understanding of your target market and what they're looking for in a property.

2. **Find the right property**: Look for properties that are in good locations, have good bones, and are priced well. It's also important to consider the potential for future

growth in the area, as this will impact the resale value of the property.

3. **Hire the right professionals**: You'll likely need to hire contractors, architects, engineers, and other professionals to help you with the development and renovation process. Make sure you choose individuals who are experienced, reliable, and who you can trust.

4. **Manage your budget**: Make sure you have a detailed budget in place, and stick to it as closely as possible. This will help you avoid overspending, and ensure that you have enough capital to complete the project.

5. Timing: Make sure that you have a solid understanding of the timeline for your project. This will help you plan your work, and make sure that everything is done in a timely manner. It's important to be realistic about the amount of time that each task will take, and to build in some extra time for unexpected delays.

6. **Planning and Design**: Make sure to carefully plan and design your renovation or development project. This will help you to identify any potential problems before they arise, and to ensure that your end product is exactly what you want. Consider working with an architect or designer to help you with this process.

7. **Contractors and Vendors**: When it comes to development and renovation work, it's important to choose the right contractors and vendors. Look for professionals with a good reputation, and make sure to get references from past clients. It's also a good idea to get several bids from different contractors, so that you can compare prices and services.

8. **Safety**: Make sure to prioritize safety during your development or renovation project. Make sure that all workers are trained in safe work practices, and that they understand the importance of following safety protocols. This will help to minimize the risk of accidents or injuries on the job.

9. **Communicate with your team**: Regular communication with your team is key to ensuring that the development and renovation process runs smoothly. Make sure everyone is on the same page, and that there is a clear understanding of what needs to be done and when.

Here's a story to illustrate these points:

Sara was a successful real estate investor who had always been interested in developing and renovating properties. She had a clear plan in mind, and was always on the lookout for properties that had potential.

One day, she found a property that was perfect for her needs. It was located in a good neighborhood, had good bones, and was priced well. She hired a team of professionals, including a contractor, an architect, and an engineer, to help her with the development and renovation process.

Sara made sure to communicate regularly with her team, and to keep a close eye on the budget. Despite a few hiccups along the way, the project was completed on time and within budget. The finished property was a huge success, and Sara was able to sell it for a significant profit.

By following these steps, Sara was able to successfully develop and renovate a property, and turn it into a profitable investment. Whether you're just starting out, or you're an experienced real estate investor, these tips can help you achieve success in the world of property development and renovation.

How to manage construction and renovation projects using practical:

Managing construction and renovation projects can be a challenging but rewarding process for real estate investors. It requires careful planning, budgeting, and coordination to ensure that the project stays on track, within budget, and meets the desired end-result. In this section, we'll take a look at the key elements of managing a successful construction or renovation project and provide practical examples filled with stories to illustrate the process.

1. **Project Planning**: Before any work can begin, a clear plan must be put in place. This involves defining the scope of the project, setting goals and timelines, and determining the budget. It's important to work with a team of professionals such as architects, engineers, and contractors to ensure that the project is feasible and that everyone is on the same page.

   For example, let's say that you have purchased a property that you plan to flip. You want to turn the outdated 2-bedroom, 1-bathroom home into a modern 3-bedroom, 2-bathroom home. To do this, you will need to work with a team of professionals to create a detailed plan for the renovation. This plan will include the scope of work, a budget, and a timeline for completion.

2. **Budgeting**: Once the plan is in place, it's time to budget for the project. This involves determining the cost of materials, labor, permits, and other expenses. It's important to be realistic about the budget, as unexpected costs can arise during the course of the project.

For example, let's say that you have budgeted $100,000 for the renovation of your property. However, during the course of the renovation, you discover that the electrical system needs to be completely replaced. This unexpected expense will add an additional $20,000 to the budget. To mitigate the impact of these unexpected costs, it's important to have a contingency budget in place.

3. **Hiring Contractors**: Once the plan and budget are in place, it's time to hire contractors to carry out the work. This involves interviewing potential contractors, reviewing their portfolios, and checking references. It's important to choose contractors who have experience in similar projects and who can work within your budget and timeline.

   For example, let's say that you have identified three potential contractors for your renovation project. After interviewing each of them and reviewing their portfolios, you choose the contractor who has the most experience in similar projects and who can work within your budget and timeline.

4. **Project Management:** Throughout the course of the project, it's important to closely manage the work being done. This involves regularly inspecting the work, ensuring that the contractors are adhering to the plan and budget, and making any necessary adjustments to the plan.

   For example, let's say that you have hired a contractor to carry out the renovation of your property. You visit the site regularly to inspect the work and ensure that the contractors are adhering to the plan and budget. If you notice any issues or deviations from the plan, you address them immediately to ensure that the project stays on track.

When it comes to managing construction and renovation projects, there are several important factors to keep in mind. First and foremost, it is important to have a clear plan and timeline for the project, as well as a budget that will allow you to complete the work in a timely and cost-effective manner. This means working with contractors, architects, and other professionals to ensure that the project stays on track and that the necessary permits and approvals are obtained.

Another important factor to consider is communication and coordination with all parties involved in the project. This includes staying in close contact with your contractors, ensuring that everyone is on the same page in terms of the project goals, and making sure that any questions or concerns are addressed promptly and effectively.

Additionally, it is important to be proactive in identifying and mitigating any potential risks or challenges that may arise during the course of the project. This may include things like weather-related delays, issues with the building's infrastructure, or unforeseen costs or complications. By staying vigilant and being prepared to adapt as needed, you can help ensure that your renovation project is a success.

A practical example of this would be a real estate investor named Mark who wanted to purchase an older property and renovate it for rental purposes. Mark found a fixer-upper in a great location, but he knew that the renovation process could be challenging. He worked with a team of contractors and architects to develop a detailed plan for the renovation, and he made sure to set aside a budget that would allow him to complete the project in a timely and cost-effective manner. Throughout the renovation process, Mark stayed in close communication with his contractors, and he was proactive in identifying and mitigating any potential risks or challenges. In the end, Mark was able to complete the renovation on time and on budget, and he was able to start generating rental income from the property shortly thereafter.

The importance of working with professionals such as architects contractors and real estate agents:

When it comes to developing and renovating properties, it's important to work with professionals such as architects, contractors, and real estate agents. This is because these professionals bring a wealth of knowledge, expertise, and resources to the table that can help make your projects run more smoothly and effectively.

Here are some practical examples that highlight the importance of working with these professionals:

1. **Working with an Architect**: Imagine you have purchased a property that you want to renovate. You have an idea of what you want the end result to look like, but you're not sure how to get there. This is where an architect comes in. An architect can help you turn your vision into a concrete plan, taking into account the local building codes and regulations. With their expertise, they can also help you identify potential structural or design issues that could impact the feasibility or cost of your renovation project.
2. **Working with a Contractor**: Once you have a solid plan in place, it's time to bring in a contractor to get the job done. A good contractor will have the experience and skills to ensure that your renovation is completed to a high standard, within budget, and on time. They will also be able

to manage the various trades and suppliers involved in the project, which can be a complex and time-consuming task for those without the necessary experience.

3. **Working with a Real Estate Agent**: If you're planning to rent out your property after the renovation is complete, it's a good idea to work with a real estate agent. An agent can help you find the right tenants for your property, negotiate lease terms, and handle all the other details of property management. They can also provide valuable insights into the local rental market, which can be helpful when setting rental rates and determining the best marketing strategies to attract tenants.

Let's take a look at some additional practical examples that illustrate the importance of working with professionals in real estate development and renovation projects:

1. *A successful real estate developer, Sarah, had always handled everything on her own, from finding properties to managing the renovation process. One day, she decided to invest in a large-scale renovation project, thinking she could save money by doing everything on her own. However, the project quickly turned into a nightmare when she realized she didn't have the expertise to deal with unexpected issues that arose during the renovation process. Sarah quickly realized the importance of working with professionals and brought in a contractor, who helped her finish the project within budget and on time.*

2. *Tom, an amateur investor, was eager to start his first renovation project but was unsure of where to start. He did a little research and decided to go it alone, thinking he could save money by avoiding professional fees. However, Tom quickly realized that he was in over his head when he encountered problems with electrical and plumbing*

systems. In the end, Tom was forced to bring in professionals to fix the problems, which ended up costing him more money in the long run. This experience taught Tom the value of working with professionals from the start to avoid costly mistakes.

3. A young couple, Rachel and Mike, bought their first investment property with the intention of fixing it up and flipping it for a profit. They thought they could handle the renovation themselves, but after tearing down walls and installing new fixtures, they found themselves struggling to complete the project. Frustrated, they hired a real estate agent to help them find a professional contractor to finish the job. The agent helped them find a reputable contractor who not only finished the renovation, but also gave them valuable advice on how to increase the value of their property.

Chapter 6:
Managing Your Properties

Congratulations on your successful investment in real estate! Now that you own properties, it's important to manage them effectively to maximize your return on investment.

Here are some key concepts and practical examples to help you in this endeavor.

1. Establishing a Rental Policy

One of the first things you should do when managing your properties is to establish a rental policy. This policy should outline the terms and conditions of tenancy, including rent amounts, security deposit requirements, and rules regarding late payment.

For example, let's say you own a rental property in a desirable area of town. You may decide to charge a higher rent to reflect the desirability of the location. Your rental policy should outline the terms of rent payments, such as due dates, grace periods, and penalties for late payment. It should also explain the consequences of not meeting the policy's requirements, such as evictions.

2. Finding and Screening Tenants

Next, it's important to find and screen tenants. You want to make sure you rent your properties to responsible tenants who will pay their rent on time and take care of the property.

For example, you may decide to work with a real estate agent who specializes in rentals. They can help you find qualified tenants, conduct background checks, and verify employment and income information. Alternatively, you may choose to advertise your property on websites such as Craigslist or Zillow.

3. Collecting Rent

Collecting rent is a critical part of managing your properties. You want to make sure that rent is paid on time and in full.

For example, you may decide to set up automatic rent payments through a service such as Plastiq or RentPayment. This makes it easy for tenants to pay their rent on time and eliminates the need for you to chase them down for payment. Alternatively, you may choose to use a property management company to collect rent and handle other aspects of property management.

4. Maintenance and Repairs

Maintaining your properties is essential to keep them in good condition and attract tenants. This includes routine upkeep as well as responding to repair requests.

For example, you may decide to handle maintenance and repairs yourself or hire a property management company to do it for you. If you choose to handle it yourself, make sure you have a good understanding of basic repairs and maintenance. You can also keep a handyman on call for emergency repairs.

5. Improving the Property

Improving your properties is a great way to increase their value and attract tenants. Whether you're adding new appliances, renovating bathrooms, or making other updates, it's important to consider the cost versus the potential return on investment.

For example, you may decide to update your properties with energy-efficient appliances and features, such as low-flow toilets, energy-efficient light bulbs, and programmable thermostats. These upgrades can help you save money on utilities and attract environmentally conscious tenants. Additionally, you can also consider making cosmetic upgrades, such as painting or adding new flooring, to improve the overall appearance of your properties.

Day-to-day management of properties:
Managing properties on a day-to-day basis can be a challenging and time-consuming task, but it is also an important part of ensuring your investments are profitable.

Here are some tips and practical examples to help you effectively manage your properties.

1. Regular Maintenance and Repairs

One of the most important aspects of property management is ensuring that the properties are well-maintained and any necessary repairs are made promptly. For example, imagine you have a rental property and one of the tenants calls to report a leaky faucet. If you don't address the issue quickly, it could lead to further damage and more costly repairs. On the other hand, if you respond promptly and fix the issue, you'll keep your tenants happy and avoid any costly repairs down the road.

2. Rent Collection

Rent collection is another important aspect of property management. It's important to establish clear payment expectations with your tenants and to follow up promptly if rent is late. For example, you could set a deadline for rent payment, such as the 5th of every month, and send out reminder emails or text messages a few days before the deadline. If a tenant misses the deadline, you could send them a friendly reminder and, if necessary, take legal action to recover the rent.

3. Communication with Tenants

Good communication with your tenants is crucial for a successful property management experience. You should be available to answer any questions or concerns your tenants may have, and respond promptly to any maintenance requests. You could also consider setting up a system for receiving and tracking maintenance requests, such as a tenant portal or a property management app.

4. Marketing and Advertising

When a tenant moves out, it's important to find a new one as quickly as possible to minimize any lost rental income. Effective marketing and advertising can help you find new tenants quickly. For example, you could list your property on popular rental websites, such as Zillow or Craigslist, or take advantage of social media advertising to reach a wider audience.

5. Record Keeping

Finally, it's important to keep accurate records of all your properties, including rental income, expenses, and maintenance records. This will help you track the performance of your properties, identify any potential problems, and make informed decisions about future investments.

6. Staying Current on Regulations: Keeping up-to-date with local, state, and federal regulations is an important aspect of property management. This includes understanding zoning laws, fair housing laws, and any other relevant regulations that may impact your properties.

Finding and Managing Tenants
Finding and managing tenants is a crucial aspect of property management. As a landlord, it is important to find tenants who will pay rent on time and take good care of the property.

Additionally, effective management of tenants helps to maintain a positive landlord-tenant relationship, minimize the risk of disputes and ensure the long-term success of your investment.

Here are a few key tips for finding and managing tenants:

1. **Screen Tenants Carefully**: It is important to screen tenants carefully to ensure they are a good fit for your property. This can include checking their credit score, employment history and rental history. You can also ask for references and conduct an interview with potential tenants.
2. **Advertise Your Property**: Make sure you advertise your property in the right places. This can include online

platforms such as Craigslist, Zillow, and Realtor.com, as well as local newspapers and community bulletin boards.

3. **Offer Attractive Amenities**: Offer attractive amenities such as on-site laundry facilities, a gym, or a pool to attract tenants. These amenities can make your property stand out from others and can also help to increase rent prices.

4. **Be Clear About Your Policies**: Be clear about your policies, such as rent payment due dates, late payment fees, and the process for requesting repairs. This can help to minimize misunderstandings and disputes down the road.

5. **Manage Maintenance and Repairs**: Ensure that maintenance and repairs are taken care of promptly. This can include fixing leaky faucets, addressing pest control issues, and making any necessary upgrades to the property.

6. **Handle Late Rent Payments and Eviction Process**: If a tenant is consistently late with rent payments, it is important to take action. This can include sending a late rent payment notice or starting the eviction process. It is important to handle these situations professionally and in accordance with your local laws and regulations.

Example 1:

John had always dreamed of being a landlord. He had finally saved up enough money to buy a rental property and was excited to start finding tenants. He had heard horror stories of tenants who didn't pay rent on time or destroyed the property, so he knew that finding the right tenants was crucial.

He started by advertising his property on several online platforms and local newspapers. He received several responses and set up several showings. He was pleasantly surprised by the number of interested parties, but he also knew that he needed to screen them carefully.

John asked each prospective tenant to fill out a rental application and he also checked their credit score and employment history. He was especially careful to check their rental history, as he didn't want any previous landlords to have negative things to say about them.

After thoroughly screening several tenants, John decided to rent to a young couple who had just relocated to the area. They both had good jobs and a positive rental history. John was confident that they would be great tenants.

John made sure to be clear about his policies, such as rent payment due dates and the process for requesting repairs. He also made sure to handle any maintenance and repair issues promptly, as he didn't want his tenants to be unhappy with their living situation.

Several months into their tenancy, John received a call from the couple, informing him that the faucet in the bathroom was leaking. John made arrangements to have it fixed as soon as possible, and the couple was very grateful

for his prompt response.

Example 2:

Finding Tenants through Networking:

Let's say you're a new real estate investor who just purchased a rental property in a bustling city. You're not exactly sure where to start in terms of finding tenants, but you know one thing for certain - you want to find the right tenant who will take care of the property and pay their rent on time. So, you attend local events and engage with people in the community. You meet a few people who are looking for a place to rent, and you give them your business card *and invite them to come check out your property. By building relationships and networking, you're able to find a tenant who not only takes great care of the property but also recommends your rental to friends and family members looking for a place to rent.*

Example 3:

Screening Tenants:

Let's say you've found a few interested tenants and you're ready to start screening them. You know it's important to find someone who will be a responsible tenant, so you do your due diligence and ask for references, run a background check, and verify their employment and income. During one tenant screening, you discover that a potential tenant has a history of not paying rent on time and has even been evicted before. By taking the time to screen your tenants, you're able to avoid potential headaches down the line and find a tenant who will treat your property with respect.

Example 4:

Communication with Tenants:

Let's say you've found your dream tenant and they're about to move in. You want to set the tone for a great landlord-tenant relationship from the start, so you make sure to communicate clearly and regularly with your tenant. You set up a system for rent payment and provide a clear expectation for maintenance and repairs. When your tenant has a maintenance issue, you respond promptly and address it in a timely manner. By taking the time to establish open and clear communication with your tenant, you're able to foster a positive relationship and ensure that your property is well-cared for.

Let's explore some additional practical examples for finding and managing tenants.

1. **Word-of-Mouth Recommendations**: Imagine you're a landlord and one of your tenants is moving out. They loved living in your property and recommend it to their friend who's also looking for a new place to live. This type of referral can be a powerful tool in finding quality tenants. Encouraging your current tenants to spread the word can bring in potential renters who are pre-screened and have a personal connection to your property.

2. **Utilizing Technology**: The internet has made it easier to find potential tenants and manage the rental process. Platforms like Zillow and Craigslist can be a great way to list your property and reach a large pool of potential tenants. You can also use property management software to automate tasks like rent collection, maintenance requests, and lease renewals.

3. **Partnering with a Real Estate Agent**: Another option to consider is partnering with a real estate agent. They have access to a large network of potential tenants, and their expertise in the local market can help you determine the best price for rent. They can also handle the advertising, showings, and application process, freeing up your time to focus on other aspects of property management.

4. **Hosting Open Houses**: Hosting an open house can be a great way to get in front of potential tenants and show off your property. Make sure to highlight the unique features of your property and be ready to answer any questions that come up. This can also be an opportunity to get a sense of who your potential tenants are, their needs and interests.

5. **Offer Incentives**: Offering incentives such as a rent-free month or a waived security deposit can be a great way to entice potential tenants to sign a lease. This can be

especially effective if you're having trouble filling a vacancy or if the rental market is particularly competitive. Just be sure to consider the financial impact of any incentives you offer and make sure it's within your budget.

Maintaining and improving the value of your properties;

Maintaining and improving the value of your properties is essential to ensure that you get the best return on your investment. There are several practical steps you can take to help you achieve this goal. Here are a few examples:

1. **Regular maintenance and upkeep**: Regular maintenance and upkeep are crucial to keep your properties in good condition. This can include things like fixing leaks, painting, and general cleaning. Regular maintenance not only keeps your properties looking good, but it can also prevent small problems from becoming big, expensive issues down the line.
2. **Renovations**: Renovating a property can be a great way to improve its value and make it more attractive to potential tenants. For example, updating the kitchen or bathroom can add a lot of value to a property and make it more appealing to tenants. However, it's important to be careful when renovating and make sure you don't over-improve the property, which can be a mistake if you plan on selling the property in the future.
3. **Rent Increases**: Regularly increasing the rent can help keep pace with rising costs and ensure that you're getting the best return on your investment. But it's important to be mindful of the local market and ensure that your rent increases are reasonable and in line with other properties in the area.
4. **Invest in the neighborhood**: Improving the neighborhood around your properties can help increase their value and make them more attractive to tenants. This could include

things like investing in local parks, supporting local businesses, and helping to maintain community events.

5. **Build a strong relationship with tenants**: Building a strong relationship with your tenants can help you maintain the value of your properties. Good tenants are more likely to take care of your properties and report problems as soon as they arise, which can prevent costly repairs in the future.

6. **Monitor the market**: Keep an eye on the real estate market and make sure you are aware of trends and changes that could impact the value of your properties.

7. **Diversify your portfolio:** Diversifying your portfolio of properties can help spread out risk and improve your overall return on investment. Consider investing in different types of properties, such as multi-family homes, commercial properties, or vacation rentals.

8. **Network with other real estate investors**: Building relationships with other real estate investors can provide you with valuable insights and ideas for maintaining and improving the value of your properties. You can also consider joining a real estate investment group or participating in local real estate events.

9. **Consider adding value-added amenities**: Consider adding value-added amenities to your properties, such as a community garden, a dog park, or a gym, to attract renters and increase the overall value of your properties.

10. **Invest in technology**: Technology can help streamline the management of your properties, and can also provide additional benefits to your tenants, such as smart home features and online rent payment systems.

Remember, the key to maximizing the value of your properties is to be proactive, stay informed, and make smart investments.

Chapter 7:
Taxation and Legal Considerations

When it comes to investing in real estate, it's important to understand the tax and legal implications of your investments. As a property owner, you'll be responsible for paying taxes on the income you earn from your rental properties, as well as for any profits you make when you sell a property. In addition, there are a number of legal considerations you'll need to take into account, including zoning laws, building codes, and tenant rights.

One practical example of the importance of understanding tax laws and regulations is for property owners who are renting out their properties. In this case, it's essential to know the tax implications of rental income, including the amount of rental income that's taxable and the deductions you can take for expenses related to the rental property.

For example, you can deduct mortgage interest, property taxes, insurance, repairs and maintenance, advertising, and other expenses incurred in the management of the rental property.

Another practical example is when you're buying and selling properties. In this case, it's important to understand the capital gains tax implications and the laws surrounding the sale of real estate. For example, when you sell a property that's appreciated in value, you'll have to pay capital gains tax on the profit you made from the sale. However, you may be eligible for certain exemptions and exclusions that can help reduce your tax liability.

In terms of legal considerations, it's crucial to understand the laws surrounding property ownership, zoning regulations, and property management. For example, you need to ensure that your properties comply with all local, state, and federal laws, including building codes, health and safety regulations, and environmental standards. You also need to understand the laws surrounding eviction, lease agreements, and other aspects of property management.

It's always recommended to consult with a tax professional and a real estate attorney to ensure that you're fully aware of the tax and legal implications of your real estate investments. This way, you can make informed decisions and avoid any potential legal or financial pitfalls down the line.

Let's take a look at some practical examples of how these factors can impact your real estate investments.

Example 1: Tax Implications

John is a real estate investor who has just purchased a rental property. He's excited to start earning passive income from his investment, but he's also a bit worried about the taxes he'll have to pay.

John learns that as a landlord, he'll be responsible for paying taxes on the rent he collects from his tenants. He'll also need to pay capital gains tax if he sells the property for a profit. To minimize his tax bill, John decides to work with a tax professional who specializes in real estate investments. With their help, he learns about tax deductions and credits that can help reduce his tax bill, such as the mortgage interest deduction and the depreciation deduction.

Example 2: Legal Considerations

Jane is a new real estate investor who has just purchased her first rental property. She's eager to start finding tenants and earning passive income, but she's also a bit nervous about all the legal requirements that come with being a landlord.

To ensure that she's in compliance with all the relevant laws and regulations, Jane decides to work with a real estate attorney. With their help, she learns about her responsibilities as a landlord, such as making sure her rental property meets all the necessary building codes and safety standards. She also learns about her obligations to her tenants, such as providing a safe and habitable living environment and respecting their privacy.

Let me give you some practical examples of tax and legal considerations for real estate investment:

1. **Depreciation:** When you own a rental property, you can take advantage of tax benefits by depreciating the property over a 27.5 year period for residential properties and 39 years for commercial properties. This helps to offset some of the costs of owning a rental property, and can lead to substantial tax savings.
2. **Tax-free exchanges**: If you have multiple investment properties, you may be able to take advantage of tax-free exchanges. This is a way of exchanging one investment property for another, without incurring any tax consequences. This can be an effective way of upgrading your investment portfolio, while minimizing your tax liability.

3. **Capital gains tax**: When you sell a property, you may be subject to capital gains tax. The amount of tax you pay will depend on a variety of factors, including your income, the length of time you held the property, and the type of property you sell. However, you may be able to reduce your tax liability by using deductions, such as depreciation and capital improvement costs, to offset some of the gain from the sale.

4. **Zoning and building codes**: When investing in real estate, it's important to consider the zoning and building codes that apply to your property. For example, if you want to convert a single-family home into a multi-unit property, you may need to obtain special permits and comply with local building codes. Failing to do so could result in fines and legal penalties.

5. **Property disputes**: Disputes over real estate can be time-consuming and expensive. Common disputes include boundary disputes, easement disputes, and disputes over property rights. To minimize the risk of disputes, it's important to have a clear understanding of the property boundaries, to obtain an accurate survey of the property, and to obtain a title insurance policy to protect your interests.

Example 1: Property tax deductions

Meet Sarah, a new real estate investor who just purchased her first rental property. She was thrilled about the income the property was generating, but soon found out that property taxes were eating into her profits. Sarah was unaware that she could deduct property taxes from her federal income tax. After consulting with her accountant, she learned that property taxes, mortgage interest, and other expenses related to the rental property could be written off as business expenses. This simple change in her tax strategy allowed Sarah to keep more of her rental income and make a better return on her investment.

Example 2: Depreciation

Tom and Jane are a married couple who recently invested in a rental property. They were surprised to learn that they could claim depreciation on the property as a tax deduction. This is because the government recognizes that the value of the property decreases over time due to wear and tear. By claiming depreciation, Tom and Jane were able to reduce their taxable income and pay less in taxes. However, it's important to note that claiming depreciation does not affect the actual value of the property, only its taxable value.

Example 3: Capital Gains Tax

John is a real estate investor who has been in the game for a few years. He recently sold one of his rental properties for a significant profit and was shocked to find out that he owed a significant amount in capital gains tax. John was unaware that when you sell a property for more than you bought it for, the profit is taxed as a capital gain. This can be a substantial amount, but there are ways to minimize it. For example, if John had held the property for more than a year, he would have qualified for a lower long-term capital gains tax rate. Additionally, he could have reinvested the profits into another rental property through a 1031 exchange and defer paying capital gains tax until he sells the new property.

These examples illustrate how taxes can significantly impact your real estate investment, but with the right strategies, you can minimize their impact. It's always a good idea to consult with a tax professional or financial advisor to ensure you are making the best decisions for your particular situation.

Here are some additional practical examples of understanding taxes on real estate investment:

1. *John and Sarah are a young couple who just bought their first rental property. They soon discovered that they have to pay property taxes on the income they earn from their rental property. They met with their accountant to understand the tax implications of their investment and learned that they have to pay federal, state and local taxes on the rental income.*
2. *Mark, an experienced real estate investor, has a portfolio of rental properties. He learned that he can deduct expenses such as mortgage interest, property tax, insurance, and repairs from his taxable rental income. This helps him lower his tax bill and increase his profits.*
3. *Rachel, a new real estate investor, was not aware of the capital gains tax implications of her investment until she sold her first rental property. She learned that she has to pay capital gains tax on the profit she made from the sale of the property. She worked with her financial advisor to understand the best strategies for reducing her capital gains tax liability.*

Legal aspects of real estate investment are crucial to understand and properly navigate to avoid potential risks and financial losses.

There are various legal considerations when investing in real estate, from purchasing a property to managing it, to selling it.

In this section, we will look at some of the key legal considerations for real estate investors and provide practical examples to illustrate their importance.

1. **Property Ownership**: One of the first legal considerations when investing in real estate is determining who owns the property. It's essential to conduct thorough research to ensure that the person or entity selling the property has the legal right to do so. A common example of a legal issue surrounding property ownership is when a property has multiple owners, and one of them wants to sell it, but the other owner does not agree. In this situation, the parties must resolve their disagreement through the legal system.

2. **Contracts**: Contracts are an essential part of real estate transactions, and it's important to understand their implications. A contract outlines the terms and conditions of a transaction and can include provisions for financing, ownership transfer, and property management. For example, a contract may specify that a buyer must pay a certain amount of money to purchase a property, or that the seller must make certain repairs before the property is transferred. If a contract is not properly drafted or executed, it may be unenforceable, which can result in financial losses for both parties.

3. **Zoning Regulations**: Zoning regulations are laws that determine how land can be used. They dictate what types of structures can be built on a piece of land, as well as how they can be used. For example, a property that is zoned for residential use may not be used for commercial purposes. Zoning regulations can impact real estate investment, as they can limit the types of properties that can be purchased or developed.

4. **Building Codes**: Building codes are regulations that ensure the safety and health of people in buildings. They dictate what types of materials can be used in construction, the size and height of buildings, and the minimum standards for

plumbing, electrical, and heating systems. For example, if a property is not up to code, it may not be safe to occupy, and the investor may need to make expensive repairs to bring it into compliance.

5. **Environmental Regulations**: Environmental regulations are laws that protect the environment and public health. They dictate how properties can be used and developed, and what types of activities can take place on them. For example, a property that is contaminated with hazardous materials may not be suitable for development, and the investor may need to undertake expensive remediation measures to make it usable.

Here are some practical examples to illustrate the legal aspects of real estate investment:

1. **Due Diligence**: Before you make an investment in real estate, it is important to conduct due diligence to understand the property's title history, zoning laws, and any liens or encumbrances that may affect your ownership.

   For example, imagine you are considering purchasing a rental property in a new area. You perform due diligence and find that the property has a lien on it for unpaid taxes. After negotiating with the seller, you decide to move forward with the purchase and pay off the lien. This due diligence helped you avoid any legal issues down the line and ensure a clear path to ownership.

2. **Contract Review**: It is also important to review all contracts and documents associated with the purchase and ownership of the property. This includes the purchase agreement, mortgage documents, and any other contracts with contractors, tenants, or lenders.

For example, imagine you are purchasing a rental property and the seller tells you the property is in good condition. However, upon review of the contract, you find that the seller is only offering a 30-day warranty on the property. This is important information to know before moving forward with the purchase, as it may impact your budget for repairs and renovations.

3. **Zoning Laws:** Zoning laws can affect the use and development of a property.
   For example, imagine you purchase a property with plans to convert it into a multi-unit rental. However, after researching the local zoning laws, you find that the property is only zoned for single-family residential use. This could impact your plans for the property and may require you to seek a variance or special use permit from the local government.

4. **Property Management Agreements**: When managing rental properties, it is important to have a clear property management agreement in place to outline the responsibilities of both the landlord and tenant.

   For example, imagine you are a landlord with several rental properties. You have a property management agreement in place for each property that outlines the responsibilities of both parties. This helps to avoid any misunderstandings or disputes with tenants and ensures everyone is on the same page when it comes to maintenance, rent collection, and any other property-related issues.

The Importance of working with lawyers and accountants:

When it comes to investing in real estate, it's not just about finding a property, securing financing, and managing tenants. There are also important legal and tax considerations to be aware of, and having professionals in these areas on your side can make all the difference.

In this section, we'll take a look at why it's important to work with lawyers and accountants, and provide some practical examples to illustrate the value they can bring to your investment.

First, let's talk about lawyers. When you're investing in real estate, you need to make sure that you're following all the legal rules and regulations. This includes everything from zoning laws to contracts, and if you don't have a good understanding of these things, you could end up facing serious legal consequences. This is where a lawyer comes in. A good real estate lawyer will be able to advise you on all the legal aspects of your investment, from negotiating contracts to dealing with disputes.

For example, let's say you're considering buying a property that's in a historic district. Before you sign the contract, you want to make sure that you'll be able to renovate the property the way you want. A lawyer can help you understand the restrictions that come with owning a property in a historic district, and advise you on what you can and can't do. This could save you a lot of time and money in the long run, as you won't have to deal with unexpected legal issues down the road.

Now, let's talk about accountants. When you're investing in real estate, it's important to keep track of your finances, as you'll need to file taxes on your investment income. But tax laws can be complicated, and if you don't have a good understanding of them, you could end up paying more in taxes than you need to. This is where an accountant comes in. A good accountant will be able to advise you on the best tax strategies for your investment, and make sure that you're taking advantage of all the deductions and credits that are available to you.

For example, let's say you're considering buying a rental property. You know that you'll be able to claim deductions for things like mortgage interest, property taxes, and depreciation, but you're not sure exactly how much you'll be able to deduct. An accountant can help you understand the tax implications of your investment, and make sure that you're taking advantage of all the deductions you're entitled to. This could save you a lot of money in taxes, and help you maximize your investment returns.

Working with lawyers and accountants can be an important part of your real estate investment strategy. These professionals can help you navigate the legal and tax aspects of your investment, and ensure that you're making informed decisions.

By taking the time to work with the right professionals, you can avoid costly mistakes and maximize the returns on your investment.

As a real estate investor, it's important to have a good understanding of the legal and financial aspects of your investments.

Working with professionals like lawyers and accountants can help you navigate the complexities of these areas and ensure that you're making informed decisions.

Here are a few more practical examples of how these professionals can help:

1. **Protecting Your Investment**: Let's say you've just purchased a rental property and want to ensure that your rights as a landlord are protected. A lawyer can help you draft a lease agreement that outlines the terms and conditions of the tenancy, including the rent amount, security deposit, and any restrictions on the use of the property. This will help ensure that you and your tenant are on the same page and can avoid any misunderstandings down the line.
2. **Navigating Zoning Laws**: If you're looking to develop a property or make major renovations, it's important to be aware of the local zoning laws. A lawyer can help you understand these laws and make sure that your proposed plans are in compliance. This can help avoid costly delays or legal issues that could negatively impact your investment.
3. **Managing Tax Implications**: Real estate investment can have a significant impact on your tax liability. An accountant can help you understand the tax implications of your investments and identify ways to minimize your tax bill. For example, if you're investing in rental properties, an accountant can help you understand the tax benefits of depreciation and help you claim any deductions you're entitled to.
4. **Handling Legal Disputes**: No matter how careful you are, legal disputes can arise in real estate investment. Whether it's a tenant-landlord dispute, a zoning issue, or a contract dispute, a lawyer can help you navigate the legal process and represent your interests in court. Having a professional on your side can help you resolve legal disputes quickly and efficiently, minimizing any disruption to your investments.

5. Contract Review: A good lawyer can review all contracts related to your investment, such as purchase contracts, rental agreements, and management contracts, to make sure you understand your obligations and protect your interests.
6. Legal Compliance: Your lawyer can also advise you on the legal requirements for owning, managing and renting properties, such as fair housing laws, health and safety codes, and tax laws. They can help you comply with these laws and avoid penalties.
7. Tax Advice: An accountant can help you understand the tax implications of your investment, such as how much you'll owe in property taxes, income taxes, and capital gains taxes. They can also help you claim tax deductions and credits to lower your tax bill.
8. Estate Planning: If you plan to pass your properties down to your heirs, your lawyer can help you create a will or trust that outlines your wishes and protects your assets.

Example: Maria is a real estate investor who recently bought her third rental property. She worked with her lawyer and accountant to review the purchase contract and rental agreement, ensure legal compliance, and plan her estate. They also helped her claim deductions and credits on her tax return, lowering her tax bill.

By working with professionals, Maria was able to make informed decisions, protect her interests, and minimize her risks. This allowed her to focus on her business and grow her portfolio with confidence.

Chapter 8:
Building Your Real Estate Portfolio

Building a real estate portfolio can be a great way to diversify your investments and potentially earn passive income. However, it can also be a complex and time-consuming process. In this chapter, we will explore the key steps involved in building a successful real estate portfolio and provide practical examples to illustrate each step.

1. Define Your Investment Goals Before you start building your portfolio: It's important to have a clear understanding of your investment goals. Are you looking to earn passive income, generate long-term growth, or a combination of both? Knowing your goals will help you determine which types of properties you should be investing in, how much risk you are willing to take, and how much money you are willing to invest.

   For example, if you're looking to generate passive income, you may want to focus on buying rental properties or commercial properties with long-term tenants. On the other hand, if you're looking for long-term growth, you may want to consider investing in properties that have the potential for appreciation.

2. Research the Real Estate Market: Once you have a clear understanding of your investment goals, it's time to research the real estate market. Start by familiarizing yourself with the local real estate market, including property prices, rental rates, and the local economy. It's also important to understand the local real estate laws and

regulations, as well as the process of buying and selling properties.

For example, you might start by researching the different neighborhoods in your area, paying close attention to the type of properties available, their prices, and rental rates. You may also want to talk to real estate agents and local property managers to get a better understanding of the local real estate market.

3. Create a Budget : Once you have a good understanding of the local real estate market, it's time to create a budget. This will help you determine how much money you can afford to invest in real estate and how much you will need to set aside for expenses such as mortgage payments, property maintenance, and property management.

   For example, if you have $100,000 to invest in real estate, you may want to allocate $50,000 for the down payment and $50,000 for closing costs and other expenses. This will give you a good starting point as you begin to build your real estate portfolio.

4. Start Small: It's important to start small when building your real estate portfolio. This will allow you to get a feel for the real estate market and learn the ropes without putting all of your money at risk. You can start by investing in a single rental property or a small commercial property and gradually adding more properties to your portfolio as you become more confident.

   For example, you might start by purchasing a small rental property in a good location. Once you have a few years of experience managing that property, you can start looking for additional properties to add to your portfolio.

5. Diversify Your Portfolio: Diversification is key when building a real estate portfolio. This means investing in different types of properties, in different locations, and with different tenants. This will help spread your risk and increase your chances of success.

For example, you might start by investing in a single-family rental property, and then add a commercial property, a multi-family property, and a vacation rental property to your portfolio. This will give you exposure to different types of real estate markets and help you weather any ups and downs in the real estate market.

Building a real estate portfolio takes time, effort, and careful planning. But with a clear understanding of your investment goals, a solid plan, and a willingness to learn and adapt, you can create a successful real estate portfolio that can generate

1. Consider the local real estate market: Before investing in a property, it's important to research the local real estate market to understand the demand for rental properties, the average rental rates, and the outlook for future growth. A real estate agent or market analysis can provide this information.
2. Manage your properties professionally: Once you have invested in properties, it's important to manage them professionally to ensure they generate steady income and increase in value over time. This includes finding and managing tenants, maintaining the properties, and making improvements as necessary.
3. Stay informed: The real estate market can change quickly, so it's important to stay informed about local and national real estate trends, changes in the tax laws, and other factors that can impact your investments. A real estate agent,

accountant, and lawyer can help you stay on top of these changes.

4. Keep accurate records: Keeping accurate records of your income and expenses is critical for tax purposes and for tracking the performance of your investments. Make sure you keep receipts for all expenses related to your properties, including mortgage interest, property taxes, insurance, repairs and maintenance, and any other expenses.

5. Taking Advantage of Compounding: Real estate investments can generate income through rental income, as well as appreciation. By having multiple properties, you can benefit from the compounding effect of these returns, as the returns from one property can help finance future investments.

6. Spreading Out Your Risk: With a larger portfolio, you can spread out the risk across multiple properties, instead of relying on the success of just one. This can help provide a safety net in case one property underperforms, as the returns from the rest of the portfolio can help offset any losses.

7. Building Wealth Over Time: Building a real estate portfolio takes time and dedication, but the long-term rewards can be substantial. By investing in properties and managing them effectively, you can grow your wealth over time, eventually leading to financial independence and stability.

8. Creating Passive Income: By building a real estate portfolio, you can create a passive income stream through rental income. This can help you build wealth without having to actively work, providing financial freedom and stability.

For example, let's say you're a young couple looking to build a real estate portfolio. You start by investing in a small rental property in a good location. Over time, you build up your portfolio by acquiring more properties and diversifying your investments. With the help of a real estate agent and a team of professionals, you manage your properties effectively and stay informed about market trends and changes in tax laws. By following these steps, you are able to build a strong and profitable real estate portfolio that provides you with a steady income and a secure future.

Strategies for diversifying your real estate investments

Diversification is a key aspect of any investment portfolio and real estate is no exception. The idea behind diversifying your investments is to spread out your risk across different asset classes and types of properties.

By doing so, you can potentially mitigate the impact of market downturns on your portfolio and enjoy more consistent returns over the long term.

Here are some practical examples of how you can diversify your real estate investments:

1. **Geographical Diversification:** Investing in properties in different geographical locations can help you diversify your portfolio and reduce the impact of local market conditions on your investments.
   For example, if you invest in a rental property in a city that's heavily reliant on one industry and that industry takes a hit, your property's value and rental income may also be affected. However, if you also invest in properties in different cities or regions, you can potentially mitigate this risk.
2. **Asset Class Diversification:** Diversifying your investments across different asset classes can also help reduce risk.

For example, you might invest in a mix of residential and commercial properties, or a mix of rental properties and real estate development projects.

3. **Property Type Diversification**: Investing in a mix of different types of properties, such as single-family homes, apartments, townhouses, and commercial buildings, can help you diversify your portfolio and potentially reduce risk.

   For example, if the demand for apartments decreases, the demand for single-family homes may still be strong, and vice versa.

4. **Tenant Diversification**: Investing in properties with a mix of tenants, such as residential and commercial tenants, can also help you diversify your portfolio and reduce risk. For example, if one of your commercial tenants goes out of business, you still have other tenants to provide a steady stream of income.

Here's a story to illustrate this point:

A couple named Bob and Susan had always been interested in real estate investing, but they were worried about the risks involved. They decided to consult a financial advisor who advised them to diversify their investments across different asset classes, property types, and geographical locations.

The couple took the advice and invested in a mix of residential and commercial properties in different cities and regions. They also invested in different types of properties, such as single-family homes, apartments, and commercial buildings. As a result, when the local real estate market took a hit in one city, the impact on their portfolio was minimized thanks to their diversification strategy.

Bob and Susan were able to enjoy consistent returns on their investments and they felt much more confident in their real estate investments. They were grateful for the advice they received and continued to diversify their investments over the years.

Here are some additional practical examples for diversifying your real estate investments.

1. **Investing in different types of properties**: Consider the story of Sarah, a seasoned real estate investor who started with single-family homes but quickly realized that it was too much work for one person to manage. She then started investing in multi-family homes, which provided her with more rental income and less maintenance. However, Sarah soon realized that multi-family homes were also affected by economic downturns, just like single-family homes. That's when she diversified further and started investing in commercial properties, such as office buildings and retail spaces. By investing in different types of properties, Sarah was able to spread out her risk and secure a stable income stream.

2. **Investing in different geographic locations**: Jim was a real estate investor who initially focused on properties in his hometown. However, after a few years, he realized that his portfolio was too heavily concentrated in one area. He was exposed to local market conditions, such as economic downturns or natural disasters, that could affect his income. To diversify, Jim started investing in properties in different states and even internationally. He found that by investing in properties in different markets, he was able to reduce his risk and secure a more stable income stream.

3. **Investing in real estate investment trusts (REITs)**: John was a real estate investor who wanted to diversify his portfolio without having to manage properties himself.

That's when he discovered real estate investment trusts (REITs). REITs are publicly traded companies that own and operate income-producing real estate properties. By investing in REITs, John was able to diversify his portfolio and invest in a variety of properties, including apartment buildings, shopping centers, and hotels, without having to manage them himself.

4. **Investing in real estate crowdfunding**: Anne was a real estate investor who was looking for a more hands-off approach to investing. That's when she discovered real estate crowdfunding. Real estate crowdfunding allows investors to pool their money together and invest in properties, typically with a lower investment minimum than traditional real estate investing. Anne found that she was able to diversify her portfolio and invest in a variety of properties, including residential and commercial properties, without having to manage them herself.

These are just a few practical examples of how real estate investors can diversify their portfolios to reduce risk and secure a more stable income stream. Remember that it's important to do your own research and seek advice from professionals before making any investment decisions.

Building and managing a portfolio of properties:
Building and managing a portfolio of properties can be a complex and challenging task, but with the right strategies, it can also be a lucrative and rewarding investment. To build and manage a successful real estate portfolio, it is important to understand the basics of property investing and to have a clear plan in place.

1. **Define your investment goals:** Before you start investing in real estate, it is important to have a clear understanding of your investment goals. Are you looking to generate

passive income, build wealth over the long term, or both? This will help you determine the type of properties you should invest in and how to structure your portfolio.

2. **Conduct thorough market research**: Once you have defined your investment goals, it's time to do some research. Start by learning about the local real estate market and identifying areas with high potential for rental income and property appreciation. This will help you make informed decisions when it comes to purchasing properties.

3. **Create a diversified portfolio**: Diversification is key when it comes to real estate investing. This means investing in different types of properties, in different locations, and with different price points. For example, you could invest in a mix of residential and commercial properties, or invest in properties in different regions of the country. This helps to mitigate risk and ensure that your portfolio is well-balanced.

4. **Build a team of professionals**: Working with a team of professionals, such as a real estate agent, a property manager, and a financial advisor, can help you navigate the complexities of property investing. These experts can provide valuable insights, guidance, and support to help you make the right decisions.

5. **Focus on property management**: Managing properties effectively is key to building a successful real estate portfolio. This involves ensuring that properties are well-maintained, that tenants are happy, and that rent is paid on time. You can also consider hiring a property manager to handle day-to-day operations and ensure that your properties are running smoothly.

6. **Continuously monitor and evaluate your portfolio**: Regularly monitoring and evaluating your real estate portfolio is crucial for ensuring its success. This includes staying up-to-date on market trends, conducting regular property inspections, and making any necessary adjustments to your portfolio.

An example of a successful real estate investor is Maria. She started investing in real estate as a way to generate passive income and build wealth over the long term. Maria conducted thorough market research, created a diversified portfolio, and built a team of professionals to support her. She also focused on property management, ensuring that her properties were well-maintained and that tenants were happy. Through continuous monitoring and evaluation, Maria has been able to grow her portfolio and achieve her investment goals.

Example 2: Karen and her husband have always been interested in real estate investments. They have been saving up for years and decided to take the leap of faith and invest in their first rental property. Karen found a charming two-bedroom, two-bathroom house in a great neighborhood. After completing some renovations and making it rental ready, Karen was able to rent the property to a young family who loved the location and the cozy feel of the house. Karen and her husband were thrilled with their first investment.

Fast forward a few years, Karen and her husband have acquired several more rental properties and have a well-diversified portfolio. They have learned the importance of finding the right tenants, maintaining their properties, and keeping track of expenses. They also have a team of professionals that they rely on, including a property manager, an accountant, and a lawyer.

Example 3: Jane always loved the idea of being a real estate investor but wasn't sure where to start. She started by reaching out to a few friends and family members who *were also interested in real estate investing. They formed a small investment group and started looking for properties to invest in together. They found a four-unit apartment building that was in need of some updates. After a few months of renovations, the building was fully leased, and the investment group was able to generate a healthy return on their investment.*

The investment group continued to grow and so did their portfolio. They diversified their investments by acquiring properties in different markets and in different asset classes. They also hired a property manager to take care of the day-to-day operations of the properties. The group has been successful in their real estate investments, and they attribute their success to their ability to work together and their willingness to learn and grow.

Building and managing a portfolio of properties can be a rewarding experience, but it requires hard work, patience, and a willingness to learn. It's important to have a well-diversified portfolio, and to work with professionals who can help you achieve your goals.

Whether you're starting alone or with a group of investors, the key to success is to take things one step at a time, and to always keep your long-term goals in mind.

Maximizing returns through effective portfolio management.

Maximizing returns through effective portfolio management is the goal of many real estate investors. By utilizing smart strategies and paying close attention to market conditions, you can optimize your investments and see the best possible returns.

Here are a few practical examples that illustrate the importance of effective portfolio management:

1. **The Turnover Tenant**: Maria was a seasoned real estate investor who owned a small portfolio of rental properties. One of her properties was in high demand and she was consistently having to turn over tenants every few months. She wasn't seeing the return on investment she expected, until she sought the advice of a property management company. They advised her to raise the rent to a market rate and implement a strict screening process for new tenants. By doing this, Maria was able to reduce her turnover rate and see an increase in monthly cash flow.

2. **The Diversified Investor**: Mark was a beginner real estate investor who wanted to diversify his portfolio. He started by investing in a single-family home, but quickly realized he was putting all of his eggs in one basket. He sought the advice of a financial advisor and together they developed a strategy to diversify his portfolio by investing in a mix of single-family homes, multi-family homes, and commercial properties. Mark was able to reduce his risk and see steady returns on his investments.

3. **The Market Timer**: Sarah was an experienced real estate investor who had a large portfolio of properties. She had a knack for timing the market and was able to buy low and sell high, consistently maximizing her returns. However, when the market shifted and property values started to decline, Sarah found herself with a portfolio full of properties that were losing value. She realized that she needed to be proactive in order to protect her investments. She sought the advice of a market analyst and together they developed a strategy to sell off properties that were losing value and invest in properties that were still appreciating. Sarah was able to turn her portfolio around and continue to see strong returns.

Practical examples to help illustrate the importance of effective portfolio management in maximizing returns.

1. *Smart portfolio rebalancing - Imagine a property investor named Mark who purchased a few rental properties in a neighborhood that was rapidly gentrifying. Over time, the value of these properties skyrocketed, making up a large portion of his overall portfolio value. However, this also increased his exposure to the risk of a market downturn in that area. To mitigate this risk, Mark decided to sell some of his properties in that area and diversify into other neighborhoods and types of properties. This smart portfolio rebalancing allowed Mark to maximize his returns by reducing his exposure to market risk.*

2. *Investing in areas with high rental demand - Let's consider another property investor named Sarah who was looking to maximize her returns. She did extensive research and found that there was high demand for rental properties in the suburbs near her city. She acquired several properties in these areas and rented them out to families who were seeking more space and a quieter lifestyle. Sarah was able to secure high rental rates and low vacancy rates, maximizing her returns on investment.*

3. *Keeping an eye on market trends - Finally, consider a property investor named David who was looking to maximize his returns. He kept a close eye on the real estate market and noticed a trend of increasing demand for properties with additional living space, such as basement apartments. David acquired several properties with basement apartments, renovated them, and rented them out. As a result, David was able to increase his rental income and maximize his returns.*

Here are a few practical examples to illustrate the importance of effective portfolio management.

Example 1: Meet "John," a real estate investor who owns several rental properties. John is a hands-on investor who wants to maximize the return on his investments. He decides to hire a property management company to handle the day-to-day operations of his properties. This allows John to focus on acquiring new properties and improving the value of his existing ones.

Example 2: "Samantha" is a real estate investor who wants to diversify her portfolio. She decides to invest in different types of properties, such as single-family homes, apartment buildings, and commercial spaces. This strategy reduces the risk of having all of her investments in one area and allows her to take advantage of different market conditions and trends.

Example 3: "Jane" is a real estate investor who is looking to maximize her returns. She decides to invest in properties that need some work and then renovates them to increase their value. Jane also conducts market research to determine the best areas to invest in and invests in properties that are in high demand.

In each of these examples, effective portfolio management played a crucial role in maximizing returns and reducing risks. Whether you are a hands-on investor or prefer to hire a property management company, it's important to have a strategy in place for managing your investments. This can include things like regularly reviewing your portfolio, conducting market research, and seeking the advice of professionals such as lawyers and accountants. With a well-managed portfolio, you can increase the value of your investments and make more informed decisions about your financial future.

Chapter 9
Conclusion and Next Steps

As you approach the end of your journey in real estate investment, it is essential to take the necessary steps to ensure your success. In this chapter, we will provide you with practical examples filled with stories, using a human conversational and engaging tone, on how to effectively wrap up your real estate investment journey and take the next steps towards success.

In conclusion, real estate investment is a lucrative opportunity that requires careful planning and execution. Throughout this guide, we have provided you with a comprehensive understanding of the various aspects of real estate investment, including finding properties, managing properties, taxes and legal considerations, building and managing a portfolio, and maximizing returns.

One practical example of wrapping up your real estate investment journey is conducting a final evaluation of your portfolio. Take a look at your properties and determine which ones are performing well and which ones are not. Evaluate the costs associated with each property and determine if it's worth keeping or if it's time to sell.

Another example of taking the next steps is to keep yourself updated on industry trends and changes. Real estate investment is a dynamic field, and it is essential to stay informed of the latest developments. Read industry publications, attend conferences, and network with other investors to stay informed and ahead of the game.

Finally, it's crucial to have a plan for the future. Whether it's expanding your portfolio, buying your dream property, or retiring comfortably, it's essential to have a clear plan in place and to regularly review and adjust it as needed.

In conclusion, real estate investment is a journey that requires careful planning, execution, and continuous learning. By following the steps outlined in this guide and incorporating practical examples and stories, you will be well on your way to building a successful real estate investment portfolio.

Summary of the key takeaways from the book:

In the world of real estate investing, there's a lot to learn and a lot to take in. That's why it's important to have a summary of the key takeaways to help you remember what's most important and to use as a reference as you move forward in your investing journey. Here are some of the most important takeaways from the book:

1. Start with a solid plan: Before you jump into the world of real estate investing, it's important to have a solid plan in place. This plan should include your goals, your budget, your timeline, and your strategy for how you'll invest.
2. Know your market: One of the most important factors in real estate investing is understanding your market. This means knowing what properties are selling for, what renters are looking for, and what the local economy is like.
3. Build a diverse portfolio: Diversification is key when it comes to real estate investing. By having a diverse portfolio, you're spreading your risk across multiple

properties and markets, which can help to minimize your exposure to loss.

4. Manage your properties effectively: Day-to-day management is crucial for the success of your real estate portfolio. This includes everything from finding and managing tenants, to maintaining and improving the value of your properties.

5. Work with professionals: Working with lawyers, accountants, and other professionals is critical when it comes to real estate investing. These experts can help you navigate the legal and financial aspects of your investments, and can provide valuable advice and support as you build and manage your portfolio.

6. Keep learning: The world of real estate investing is constantly changing, and there's always more to learn. Make a commitment to continually educate yourself, whether it's through reading books, attending seminars, or networking with other investors.

7. Stay focused and disciplined: Real estate investing can be challenging at times, but it's important to stay focused and disciplined if you want to be successful. This means sticking to your plan, managing your properties effectively, and always keeping your long-term goals in mind.

By following these key takeaways and continually learning and growing as an investor, you can set yourself up for success in the world of real estate investing. So get out there, start building your portfolio, and see where the journey takes you!

Recommendation for further education and resources

When it comes to real estate investment, education and resources are key to success. No matter how much you learn, there is always more to know and more opportunities to grow your wealth. Here are some recommendations for further education and resources to help you continue on your real estate investing journey:

1. Read more books: There is no shortage of books on real estate investment, and it is always a good idea to continue learning and expanding your knowledge base. Consider books on specific areas of real estate investing, such as commercial properties, fix-and-flips, or property management.
2. Attend workshops and seminars: Workshops and seminars can be a great way to learn from experienced real estate investors and to network with others in the industry. You can find events in your area through local real estate investment clubs or online.
3. Join a real estate investment club: Real estate investment clubs are groups of like-minded individuals who come together to learn, network, and invest in real estate. You can find a club in your area by searching online or through your local real estate association.
4. Find a mentor: A mentor can be a valuable resource for learning and growing as a real estate investor. Look for someone who has experience in the areas you are interested in and who is willing to share their knowledge and experience with you.
5. Utilize online resources: The internet is a wealth of information on real estate investment, and there are many websites and forums dedicated to the subject. Consider joining online communities and participating in discussions to stay up-to-date on the latest news and trends in real estate investment.

Final thoughts and encouragement for taking action

As you come to the end of your journey in learning about real estate investment, it's time to take action. You've learned about the importance of market research, finding the right properties, managing your investments, understanding taxes and legal considerations, building your portfolio, and maximizing your returns. Now, it's time to put this knowledge into practice.

Don't be afraid to start small and gradually grow your portfolio over time. Remember, successful real estate investing takes patience, persistence, and a commitment to ongoing education. Surround yourself with knowledgeable and experienced professionals, including real estate agents, lawyers, and accountants. Keep up with the latest market trends, read industry publications, and attend events and seminars.

Most importantly, trust your instincts and be confident in your decisions. Real estate investment can be a rewarding and lucrative venture, but it's also important to understand the risks involved. Take calculated risks, and always have a plan for both success and failure.

Finally, don't let fear hold you back from pursuing your real estate investment dreams. If you've done your research, consulted with professionals, and have a solid plan in place, there's no reason why you can't be successful. So, take the next step and start building your real estate portfolio today!